AFGHANISTAN
the land

Erinn Banting

A Bobbie Kalman Book

The Lands, Peoples, and Cultures Series

Crabtree Publishing Company

www.crabtreebooks.com

The Lands, Peoples, and Cultures Series

Created by Bobbie Kalman

Coordinating editor
Ellen Rodger

Production coordinator
Rosie Gowsell

Project editor
Carrie Gleason

Project development, design, editing, and photo editing
First Folio Resource Group, Inc.
    Erinn Banting
    Tom Dart
    Greg Duhaney
    Jaimie Nathan
    Debbie Smith

Photo research
Image Select International Ltd/UK

Prepress and printing
Worzalla Publishing Company

Consultants
S. Irtiza Hasan, Muslim Students Association at the University of Houston; Mohammad Masoom Hotak

Photographs
AFP/Corbis/Magma: p. 19 (top), p. 20 (right); Paul Alamasy/Corbis/Magma: p. 18 (bottom), p. 19 (bottom), p. 22 (right); Alamy/F. Jackson: p. 25; All Over Press (Norway)/Gamma: title page; American Geographical Society Library, University of Wisconsin-Milwaukee Libraries: p. 9 (top); Heather Angel: p. 30 (both), p. 31 (both); AP Photo/Adam Butler: p. 23 (bottom), p. 27 (bottom); AP Photo/Victor R. Caivano: p. 24; AP Photo/John Moore: p. 16 (left); AP Photo/Vahid Salemi: p. 5 (bottom); AP Photo/Tomas van Houtryve: p. 29; Art Directors and TRIP/S. Maines: p. 4 (top); Art Directors and TRIP/R. Zampese: p. 20 (left); Ric Ergenbright: cover, p. 4 (bottom), p. 9 (bottom), p. 26 (right), p. 28 (bottom); Ric Ergenbright/Corbis/Magma: p. 8, p. 27 (top); Harrison Forman: p. 6; O'Malley Heathcliff/FSP/Gamma: p. 12; Doranne Jabobson: p. 3, p. 21 (top); Quidu Noel/Gamma: p. 15; Luke Powell: p. 17 (bottom); Caroline Penn/Corbis/Magma: p. 26 (left); Luke Powell: p. 21 (bottom); Carl and Ann Purcell/Painet: p. 10 (bottom), p. 11 (top); Reuters NewMedia Inc./Corbis/Magma: p. 11 (bottom), p. 13 (top), p. 22 (left); Rex Features: p. 10 (top), p. 28 (top); Reza/Webistan/Corbis/Magma: p. 5 (top), p. 13 (bottom); Patrick Robert/Corbis/Magma: p. 14, p. 23 (top); Topham Picturepoint: p. 7 (right), p. 18 (top); Peter Turnley/Corbis/Magma: p. 16 (right); Photo Courtesy of UNOCHA, Islamabad (David Edwards): p. 17 (top); Roger Wood/Corbis/Magma: p. 7 (left)

Every effort has been made to obtain the appropriate credit and full copyright clearance for all images in this book. Any oversights, despite Crabtree's greatest precautions, will be corrected in future editions.

Map
Jim Chernishenko

Illustrations
Dianne Eastman: icon
David Wysotski, Allure Illustrations: back cover

Cover: Water from a stream rushes through the Hindu Kush Mountains. People use donkeys, camels, and yaks to travel through the mountains.

Icon: Wheat, which appears at the head of each section, is the most common crop grown in Afghanistan. Once wheat is harvested, it is ground into flour at local mills and used to make many foods, such as *naan*, a type of bread that people eat with every meal.

Title page: The cool waters of the Panjsher River are a good place for a swim on a hot day. People rely on the river to irrigate their crops and to supply them with water for cooking and bathing.

Back cover: A dromedary is a type of camel with one hump. Camels have adapted to Afghanistan's harsh desert climate. They can survive on very little water, they have thick pads on their legs that allow them to kneel in the hot desert sand, and they can close their nostrils to avoid getting dust in their noses.

Published by
Crabtree Publishing Company

PMB 16A,	612 Welland Avenue	73 Lime Walk
350 Fifth Avenue	St. Catharines	Headington
Suite 3308	Ontario, Canada	Oxford OX3 7AD
New York	L2M 5V6	United Kingdom
N.Y. 10118		

Cataloging in Publication Data
Banting, Erinn.
    Afghanistan. The land / Erinn Banting.
    p. cm. -- (Lands, peoples, cultures series)
Includes index.
    ISBN 0-7787-9335-4 (RLB) -- ISBN 0-7787-9703-1 (PB)
    1. Afghanistan--Geography and climate--Juvenile literature. [1. Afghanistan] I. Title. II. Lands, peoples, and cultures series.
    DS354.B35 2003
    j958.1
                                            2003001263
                                            LC

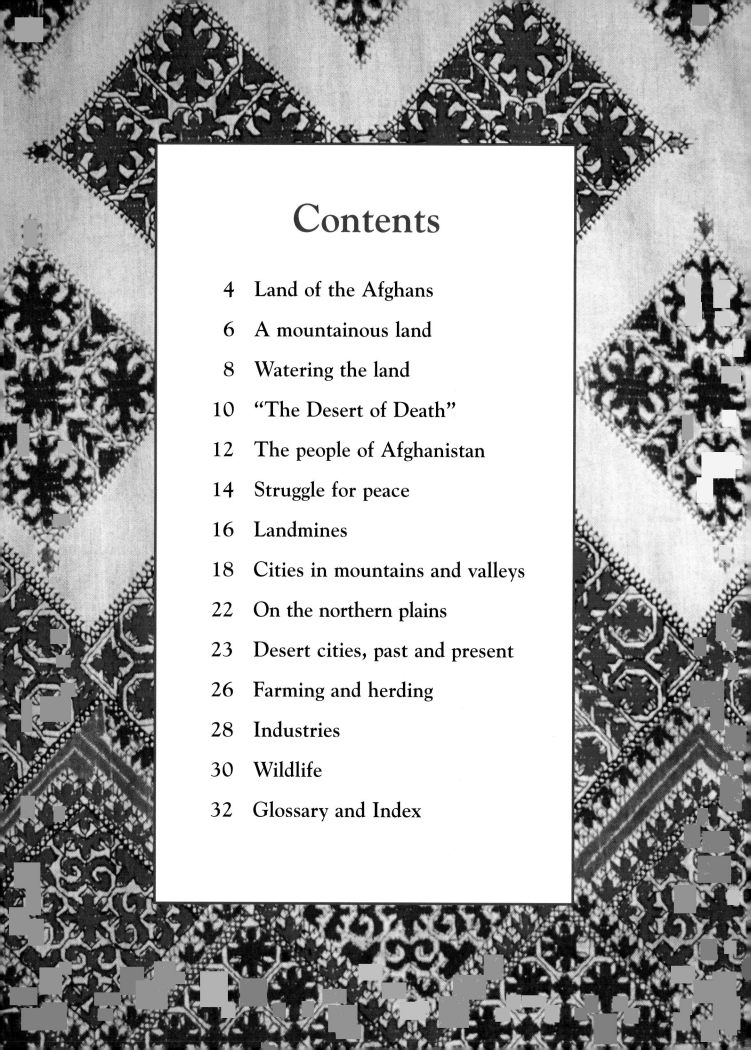

Contents

 # Land of the Afghans

"Afghanistan" means "Land of the Afghans" in Pashto and Dari, the country's two main languages. Located in central Asia, Afghanistan is bordered by Iran to the west; Turkmenistan, Uzbekistan, and Tajikistan to the north; China to the northeast; and Pakistan to the east and south. The country is landlocked, which means that not one major body of water touches its borders.

Rolling hills and **plains** dominate the northern and northwestern parts of Afghanistan, while tall mountains rise in the northeast. The country's main mountain range, the Hindu Kush, begins in the northeast and runs south to the center of the country. Dry, dangerous deserts and lowlands separated by valleys lie south of the Hindu Kush and in parts of western Afghanistan. Across this varied landscape are **shrines**, where people pray; markets in cities and villages; and *samawars*, which are small homes or restaurants where travelers and traders rest along their journeys.

(left) Sparse shrubs grow on the banks of a reservoir near Sarobi, a village in the northeast. Reservoirs are man-made ponds or lakes where water is stored.

(top) Afghanistan's mountains have many hidden caves. Some formed naturally, but others were made by soldiers as a place to hide and to store military supplies.

If this family gets tired during its long journey through the mountains, it may stop at a samawar to rest.

A land in turmoil

Narrow passes, or passages, running through the Hindu Kush link eastern and western **civilizations**. For thousands of years, **invaders** from other countries have marched through Afghanistan's deserts and mountains to gain control of the passes. Then, they used the passes for military attacks or trade routes. The Afghans have fought back, trying to keep these invaders from taking complete control of their land.

Men pray outside the Masjid-i-Jami, or Friday Mosque, in the western city of Herat. It is called the Friday Mosque because of the special prayers that Muslims say there on Fridays.

A mountainous land

The snowy peaks of the Hindu Kush tower above a forested valley.

Afghanistan is one of the highest countries in the world. Almost half the land lies at an altitude of more than 6,560 feet (2,000 meters). Nestled in the narrow valleys between the mountains are many of Afghanistan's main villages and cities. Glaciers, or slow moving chunks of ice, cover many mountain peaks and steep mountain faces.

The mighty Hindu Kush

The Hindu Kush is an extension of the Himalaya Mountains, which contain some of the highest peaks in the world. Dense forests of cedar, pine, and fir cover some parts of the mountain range, while only scrub bushes and thick grasses grow in other parts. Clinging to the rocky cliff faces are small villages and walled-in groups of buildings, called compounds, where one or more families lives.

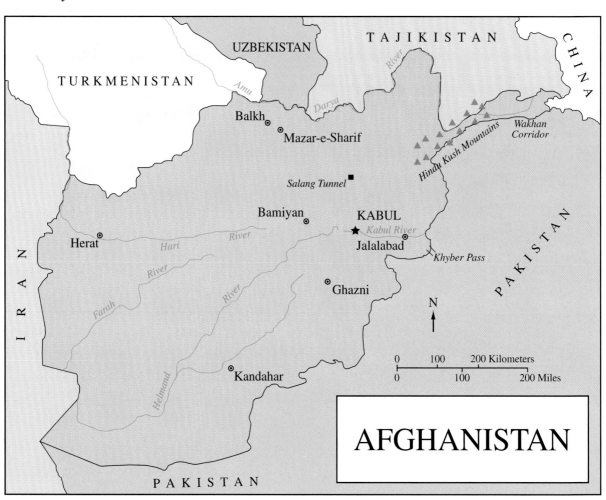

AFGHANISTAN

A colorfully painted bus winds its way along a mountain road. Many roads in Afghanistan's mountains are being repaired after they were damaged by years of war.

Wakhan Corridor

In northeastern Afghanistan, a narrow strip of land, called the Wakhan Corridor, connects the the Hindu Kush, Pamir, and Karakoram mountain ranges. The Wakhan Corridor's main village, Qal'eh-ye Panjeh, sits in a rugged valley. The village is inhabited by the Kirghiz people, who came to Afghanistan from Russia. **Nomadic** Kirghiz also live in the Wakhan Corridor. They herd yaks and live in collapsible, dome-shaped tents called yurts. The Wakhan Corridor is very far from the rest of the country, and the people who live there are isolated from other Afghans.

Mountain passes

Mountain passes connect different parts of Afghanistan with one another, and connect Afghanistan with other countries. The 33-mile- (55-kilometer-) long Khyber Pass, in the east, winds its way through an offshoot of the Hindu Kush Mountains called the Safid Koh Mountains. Two roads run through the pass, one for cars, trucks, and buses, and the other for camel **caravans**. The Khyber Pass connects Kabul, Afghanistan's capital, with Peshawar, a city in northern Pakistan.

The Shibar Pass was once a narrow pass that connected the eastern city of Kabul with the northern plains. In 1964, it was replaced by the Salang Tunnel, which runs through the mountains for nearly 1.7 miles (3 kilometers). The Salang Tunnel was the country's first year-round direct link between the north and south. The tunnel was damaged in the 1990s by fighting, but was reopened in 2002.

Mountain climate

Winters in Afghanistan are very cold. Snow and freezing winds, called scimitars, whip through the peaks and narrow gorges. Many mountain roads are completely blocked because of heavy snowfall. Winds blow in the summer, too. These winds, called monsoons, bring warm rain, especially to the northern region of Nuristan and around Jalalabad, a city in the east.

Rockfalls and earthquakes

Rockfalls are common in the mountains because of extreme changes in temperature from day to night. Heat during the day causes the mountains' rock to expand, or get larger. Below freezing temperatures at night cause the rock to contract, or get smaller. With the constant expansion and contraction, rocks shatter and tumble down the sides of mountains, blocking passes and making travel very dangerous. Massive earthquakes are also common in the Hindu Kush. Thousands of people died during earthquakes in 1998 and 2002.

The twists and turns of the Khyber Pass are difficult to navigate.

Watering the land

Most of Afghanistan's water comes from the Hindu Kush Mountains. Rain in the mountains and melted water from glaciers feed the country's streams and rivers. Afghanistan's main rivers are the Kabul, Amu Darya, Hari, and Helmand. Of these, only the Kabul and Amu Darya reach the sea. The Kabul flows east into the Indus River, in Pakistan, and then into the Arabian Sea. The Amu Darya flows west along Afghanistan's northern border, into the Aral Sea. Most of the country's other rivers empty into lakes or dry up in the hot deserts.

The Band-i-Amir, or "Dam of the Kings," is a series of six lakes in the northern mountains. These turquoise and green lakes formed in basins that are naturally dammed, or blocked, by deposits of sulfur, a type of mineral.

The Amu Darya

At 1,500 miles (2,415 kilometers), the Amu Darya is the longest river in central Asia. In ancient times, invaders and traders traveled on the river, which was then called the Oxus River, and along its shores. The Amu Darya was part of the Silk Road, a trade route that linked China and Rome. The traders carried wool, gold, and silver from the west and silk and spices from the east. Along their journey, they passed beautiful cities and mines of lapis lazuli, a type of gemstone, beside the river.

Sources of life

Afghanistan's rivers provide people, animals, and crops with water to survive. In the spring, parts of the Helmand River overflow, creating lush marshes and shallow lakes where larks, plovers, ducks, swans, and geese gather. On the **fertile** banks of the Amu Darya, farmers grow wheat and other crops, which they sell in town bazaars. The waters of the Panjsher River, a **tributary** of the Kabul River, provide water for mulberry, cherry, and apple trees to grow in the Panjsher Valley. The trees grow on terraced fields, which look like large steps climbing the sides of the Hindu Kush Mountains.

The Helmand Valley Project

The Helmand Valley Project was a massive **irrigation** project that began in the 1950s in southwestern Afghanistan. The project, which cost Afghans more than $110 million, failed. The irrigated land became so full of water that salt deep in the ground rose to the surface and made the soil unsuitable for farming. Scientists have begun to work on the project again and are trying to solve the problems in the original plan.

Dams are built across waterways, such as rivers, to control the flow of water. Modern dams, such as this one, are replacing older systems of irrigation in many parts of Afghanistan.

Irrigation

In parts of eastern, southern, and southwestern Afghanistan, an ancient system of irrigation, called *karez*, brings water to villages and farmers' fields. A *karez* is a series of wells that are connected by a tunnel and that draw water from a river. The well **shafts** are dug deep into the ground to keep the water from **evaporating**. Landowners hire four-person teams, called *karez-kan*, to replace wells that have collapsed and to clean earth and sand out of the *karez* each year. The job is very dangerous because the wells sometimes collapse while the workers are digging.

In other parts of Afghanistan, water from rivers flows along canals to irrigate the land. Dams built across the rivers control the flow of water. Many of Afghanistan's irrigation systems have been damaged by war. Regions that are no longer irrigated, such as Baghlan, a province in the north, are now unable to produce crops or vegetation.

Fields in the Bamiyan Valley, northwest of Kabul, are irrigated with karez. *The water comes from small streams in the mountains.*

"The Desert of Death"

Sand dunes in the Registan Desert reach heights of 100 feet (30 meters). The name "Registan" comes from a Persian word that means "country of sand."

Only the most skilled traveler can survive in the Dasht-i-Margo Desert, in the southwest. The stony desert is nicknamed "the Desert of Death" because so many people have died trying to cross it. The Dasht-i-Margo is the third largest desert in Afghanistan. The largest and second largest deserts are the sandy Registan, in the south, and the stony Dasht-i-Kash, in the southwest.

The Sistan Basin

Lying between the deserts is the Sistan Basin. The bowl-shaped basin, where an ancient civilization flourished until the 1300s, once held water. Now, it is a semi-desert region where very little grows. The very dry region of Gawd-i-Zirreh, in the southwest, is a salt pan, which is a hollow in the earth. The bottom of the hollow is so flat that it floods even when a small amount of rain falls. The flooding brings salt from beneath the sandy soil to the surface. When the water evaporates, the salt turns pink or white and forms a hard crust.

A dromedary, or one-humped camel, searches for water near ancient ruins that have been worn away by wind and blowing sand. There were once many settlements in the desert, but a lack of water forced people to abandon them.

Dams are built across waterways, such as rivers, to control the flow of water. Modern dams, such as this one, are replacing older systems of irrigation in many parts of Afghanistan.

Irrigation

In parts of eastern, southern, and southwestern Afghanistan, an ancient system of irrigation, called *karez*, brings water to villages and farmers' fields. A *karez* is a series of wells that are connected by a tunnel and that draw water from a river. The well **shafts** are dug deep into the ground to keep the water from **evaporating**. Landowners hire four-person teams, called *karez-kan*, to replace wells that have collapsed and to clean earth and sand out of the *karez* each year. The job is very dangerous because the wells sometimes collapse while the workers are digging.

In other parts of Afghanistan, water from rivers flows along canals to irrigate the land. Dams built across the rivers control the flow of water. Many of Afghanistan's irrigation systems have been damaged by war. Regions that are no longer irrigated, such as Baghlan, a province in the north, are now unable to produce crops or vegetation.

Fields in the Bamiyan Valley, northwest of Kabul, are irrigated with karez. *The water comes from small streams in the mountains.*

"The Desert of Death"

Sand dunes in the Registan Desert reach heights of 100 feet (30 meters). The name "Registan" comes from a Persian word that means "country of sand."

Only the most skilled traveler can survive in the Dasht-i-Margo Desert, in the southwest. The stony desert is nicknamed "the Desert of Death" because so many people have died trying to cross it. The Dasht-i-Margo is the third largest desert in Afghanistan. The largest and second largest deserts are the sandy Registan, in the south, and the stony Dasht-i-Kash, in the southwest.

The Sistan Basin

Lying between the deserts is the Sistan Basin. The bowl-shaped basin, where an ancient civilization flourished until the 1300s, once held water. Now, it is a semi-desert region where very little grows. The very dry region of Gawd-i-Zirreh, in the southwest, is a salt pan, which is a hollow in the earth. The bottom of the hollow is so flat that it floods even when a small amount of rain falls. The flooding brings salt from beneath the sandy soil to the surface. When the water evaporates, the salt turns pink or white and forms a hard crust.

A dromedary, or one-humped camel, searches for water near ancient ruins that have been worn away by wind and blowing sand. There were once many settlements in the desert, but a lack of water forced people to abandon them.

A nomadic man and his yak travel through the southern deserts. Many nomadic groups settle in the deserts during the winter, in areas with shrubs and grasses for their animals.

Desert weather

Temperatures in the desert soar to 120° Fahrenheit (50° Celsius) in the summer and plunge below 32° Fahrenheit (0° Celsius) in the winter. Rainfall is rare, but some places, such as the province of Nimroz, in the southwest, are drier than others. In Nimroz there is an average of only two inches (five centimeters) of rainfall each year.

In the Dasht-i-Margo, the *bad-i-sad-o-bist-roz*, or "wind of 120 days," blows 60 to 110 miles (100 to 180 kilometers) per hour between July and September. The wind whips up sand, making it very difficult to see. For this reason, it is sometimes called "the black wind." A similar wind, the *khakbad*, blows dust and sand around like mini-tornadoes in the southern deserts.

Travel in the desert

Most people in the desert travel by horse or camel. Some people, especially nomadic peoples, travel in camel caravans. They move from camp to camp, transporting their food, blankets, tents, and other supplies on camels. In the past, camel caravans were thousands of camels long. Today, they are much shorter.

Not many people drive in the desert because there are so few roads. People who do drive bring extra gasoline, tires, and other supplies since they never know where the next gas station will be.

Camels are used as pack animals because they can carry heavy loads.

The people of Afghanistan

Each region of Afghanistan is home to a different ethnic group, which has its own traditions, language, and history. Most groups are also found in neighboring countries, in even greater numbers than in Afghanistan. For example, the Pashtuns in Afghanistan are part of a larger group called the Pathans in Pakistan.

No matter what group Afghans belong to, most are Muslim. Muslims follow the religion of Islam. They believe in one God, Allah, and follow the teachings of his **prophet** Muhammad. The two main groups of Muslims are Sunni and Shia. Sunnis and Shias share many of the same beliefs, but have different ideas about who the leaders of Islam are.

(top) A woman wearing a chadri *holds her son at a market in Kabul. A* chadri *is a long cloak-like garment that Afghan women wear.*

Pashtuns

The Pashtuns are the largest ethnic group in Afghanistan. They live mainly in a crescent-shaped region that stretches along Afghanistan's eastern border, down through the south, and up the western border almost to Herat. All Pashtuns speak Pashto, and most are Sunni Muslims.

There are many tribes of Pashtuns. The largest are the Durrani and Ghilzai. The Durrani live in the southern deserts and around the city of Kandahar, in the southeast. Some are nomadic herders, but most work in businesses, often trading tea, spices, and handmade carpets for fruit, vegetables, and grain. The Ghilzai were once all nomadic, traveling with their sheep and cattle in search of grazing land. Today, most Ghilzai live in small villages between Kandahar and Kabul, where they work as farmers, traders, or craftspeople.

Tajiks

The second largest group in Afghanistan are the Tajiks, who also live in the neighboring country of Tajikistan. The Tajiks in Afghanistan are mainly Sunni and speak Dari. Some live in villages in the mountainous northeast, where they farm the land. Others live on the plains in northern Afghanistan, in the cities of Kabul and Herat, and in the central town of Bamiyan. They work mainly as craftspeople or traders.

Hazaras

Hazaras are Afghanistan's third largest group. They are mostly Shias who speak Hazaragi, which is a dialect, or version, of Dari. Hazaras live mainly in the mountains and narrow valleys in the center of the country, in an area called Hazarajat. Their homes are made from mud or stone, and their villages are surrounded by mud walls. They have built extensive irrigation systems through their region, which allow them to farm and raise **livestock**. Many Hazaras have moved to cities such as Kabul because of overcrowding in their region and a lack of food and jobs.

A Tajik man prays outside a mosque in Herat.

Uzbeks

Uzbeks live along Afghanistan's border with Uzbekistan, as well as in Uzbekistan. Most Uzbeks are Sunni Muslims. They work as farmers, traders, or craftspeople, communicating with one another in Uzbeki.

Many Uzbek men wear long turbans, called lungees, *to keep themselves warm and to protect them from strong winds in the mountains.*

Struggle for peace

Throughout its history, invaders and warring ethnic groups have struggled for control of Afghanistan. In 1747, the Durrani tribe of Pashtuns united the country. Their royal family ruled until Afghanistan's last king, Zahir Shah, was overthrown by his cousin and brother-in-law, Mohammed Daoud Khan, in 1973.

The PDPA

Daoud Khan faced a great deal of opposition from various Afghan tribes who wanted control of the country, and from people who did not want him to modernize Afghanistan. The opposition increased, and Daoud Khan was killed in a **coup** in 1978. A **communist** group called the People's Democratic Party of Afghanistan (PDPA) took control of the country.

Soviet invasion

When the PDPA started making changes to the way Afghanistan was run, fighting broke out in many parts of the country. The Mujahiddin, or "holy warriors," were among those who fought against the PDPA because they believed that the PDPA's changes went against the teachings of Islam. The Soviet Union sent money and weapons to help the PDPA, while the United States sent money and weapons to help the Mujahiddin. On December 24, 1979, the Soviet Union invaded Afghanistan. Many years of fighting followed. A cease-fire, or end to the fighting, was finally declared in 1988, and the last Soviet troops left Afghanistan in 1989.

Beyond Soviet rule

Problems in Afghanistan did not end when the Soviets left because they still had a great deal of support. The Mujahiddin also had strong support, especially in the countryside. Battles frequently broke out between communist supporters and the Mujahiddin. Ethnic groups also battled one another for control of different regions.

The last Soviet troops withdrew from Afghanistan in 1989.

Civil war

Support for the Mujahiddin grew, and they overthrew the Afghan government in 1992. Groups within the Mujahiddin fought among themselves because they could not agree on who should control the country, and a civil war broke out.

Growth of the Taliban

In 1995, a group of young Pashtun students began to fight for peace in Afghanistan, while teaching people about their view of Islam. They were known as the Talibs, or "students of Islam." The Talibs formed a group called the Taliban, which gained control of parts of Afghanistan. They brought stability to places that had been destroyed by years of war, but they also introduced laws that severely restricted people's rights, especially those of women and non-Pashtuns. Many of these laws were based on misinterpretations of Islam and the *Shari'ah*, which is Muslim law.

In 1996, the Taliban took control of Kabul. They brutally murdered the former president Mohammad Najibullah and hanged him in public as a warning to anyone who opposed the Taliban. Over the next few years, the Taliban gained control of even more of the country.

End of Taliban rule

The Taliban's rule ended in 2001 after the United States declared a war against **terrorists** in Afghanistan. The war began after attacks in the United States on September 11, 2001. Thousands of people were killed when terrorists flew planes into the Pentagon, in Washington, and into the World Trade Center, in New York City, and when hijacked passengers crashed their plane in Pennsylvania.

The United States suspected that the terrorist attacks were organized by Osama bin Laden, a Saudi Arabian who they believed was hiding in Afghanistan, protected by the Taliban government. With the help of the Northern Alliance, an Afghan group that opposed the

Soldiers from the United States army and members of the Northern Alliance prepare to enter Taliban-controlled Kabul in 2001.

Taliban and that occupied parts of the north during Taliban rule, the United States and its **allies** overthrew the Taliban government. Today, organizations in Afghanistan and volunteers from other countries are working to restore the rights of Afghanistan's people and repair the damage caused by decades of fighting.

Refugees

Years of fighting forced millions of Afghans to flee their country. In Pakistan, Iran, Turkmenistan, Uzbekistan, and Tajikistan, Afghan **refugees** live in camps where they have few belongings, little food and water, and poor shelter. Jalozai is one of the largest refugee camps in Pakistan. It is located near the border town of Peshawar. More than 50,000 Afghans fled to the camp after the attacks on the United States on September 11. Many Afghans are just now returning to their **homeland** with the hope of peace. The challenges they face include finding new homes and jobs.

Landmines

One of the most devastating and lasting effects of war in Afghanistan are landmines and unexploded bombs, such as cluster bombs. Landmines are weapons that are buried in the ground or covered with dirt, sand, and plants. They detonate, or explode, when something or someone puts pressure on them. Cluster bombs, which contain hundreds of tiny bomblets, are released from planes in mid-air and explode when they hit the ground. Not all the bomblets detonate, though, so people who touch them or step on them can be injured or killed. Children suffer the most from landmines and cluster bombs because they are attracted to the interesting shapes and colors.

A landmine pokes out of the ground in the Afghan countryside. Afghanistan is the most heavily mined country in the world, with an estimated five to seven million mines.

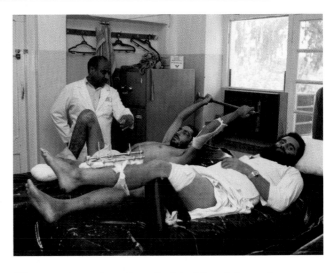

Two men rest in a hospital in Kandahar after being injured by landmines. Many people injured by landmines lose their arms or legs.

Why landmines are used

Countries at war use landmines to restrict the movement of civilians, who are people not in military service, and enemies. Most often, civilians are the ones harmed by landmines. In 1999, between 600 and 720 Afghans were killed or injured each month because of landmines. By 2000, this figure had dropped to 88 Afghans per month, but this is still too many.

Demining

The Soviets and the Mujahiddin planted most of the landmines over the last 30 years. The mines still pose a danger because they remain active for at least 50 years. The **United Nations'** Mine Action Program for Afghanistan (MAPA) is in charge of demining the country. MAPA locates and destroys active mines, and educates Afghans about the danger.

Locating and destroying mines is very difficult and time-consuming work. Deminers use a combination of methods to clear the land. They locate metal mines with metal detectors and sharp sticks. Trained dogs detect plastic mines by smelling for chemicals. Special machinery is also used to dig up mines and force them to explode.

An armored backhoe digs up landmines buried in a canal. The backhoe has special glass and metal that protects the area where the driver sits in case a landmine explodes as it is dug up.

A deminer slowly approaches a mine so he can attach an explosive device to it. He will detonate the mine once he is out of harm's way.

Cities in mountains and valleys

Cities in Afghanistan's mountains and valleys have been inhabited for thousands of years, but many of their beautiful buildings and monuments were destroyed by invasions and wars. In neighborhoods, boards cover windows shattered by gunfire, and people on foot or in buses travel on roads filled with potholes. Slowly, Afghans are trying to rebuild their cities by restoring older buildings and constructing new ones.

Shops, people, and vehicles crowd the banks of the Kabul River.

Kabul

Kabul, Afghanistan's largest city, has been inhabited for 3,500 years. It became the capital of the country in 1776. Located on the banks of the Kabul River, in a valley of the Hindu Kush, Kabul was invaded many times because it controlled mountain passes connecting the northern and southern parts of the country. In ancient times, it was also a main stop for traders traveling along the Silk Road. Many kings and leaders made their home in Kabul. They built fortresses and **mosques** there, including Kabul's main mosque, the Kabul-Eid-Gamsoque.

Divided by water

The Kabul River divides the city in two. The old city, in the south, was once home to magnificent buildings, such as the Darulaman and Chihilsotun palaces. Now, many of its buildings stand in ruin. The modern section, in the north, is home to government buildings, banks, colleges, and universities, such as the Kabul University.

The remains of the Bala Hisar fortress, which once protected the old part of Kabul, overlook the city. Today, people are not allowed near the ruins because unexploded landmines make them unsafe.

Large crowds gather to worship at the White Mosque in Jalalabad.

Jalalabad

The city of Jalalabad is built on a site where people have lived since 100 B.C. Located near the Khyber Pass, it became an important military base in the 1500s. Soldiers stationed there protected the country against invaders entering through the pass. Today, Jalalabad is known as a winter resort for wealthy Afghans because of its warm weather year-round. The city is surrounded by irrigated fields where almonds, rice, sugar cane, and fruits, such as oranges, grow. Jalalabad also has factories where sugar cane is made into white sugar, and paper-making industries.

Ghazni

Ghazni, in the east, is the only city in Afghanistan still surrounded by its original wall. The city was the capital of the Ghaznavid Empire, Afghanistan's first Muslim **dynasty**, in the 1000s. Remains of a palace built during that time can still be seen. The palace had a large, open rectangular court paved with marble; a mosque with marble floors; government offices; and quarters for soldiers.

Ghazni has been a center of commerce and industry since the 1400s. It is famous for its central market where people buy and trade livestock, furs, silk, embroidered sheepskin coats, fruits, vegetables, and grains. Visitors to its **citadel**, constructed in the 1200s, look up at the tall mud-brick walls and semi-circular bastions, from which defenders fired at attackers.

The tomb of Mahmud, who ruled Ghazni from 998 to 1030 A.D., was once covered in colorful tiles.

(left) Bamiyan was once an important religious center. Followers of the Buddhist religion lived in caves carved into the mountains.

(below) Afghans, as well as communities around the world, hope that one day the Buddhas of Bamiyan will be restored.

Bamiyan

The town of Bamiyan is northwest of Kabul. For centuries, it was an important *serai*, or resting place, for traders and merchants who traveled the Silk Road in camel caravans. From about 100 to 700 A.D., the Bamiyan Valley was also a center for Buddhism. Buddhists follow the teachings of Siddhartha Gautama, who became known as "the Buddha," which means "the Enlightened One." Buddhists believe that people are reincarnated, or born again, and that the way a person behaves in one life will determine what his or her next life will be like.

The Buddhas of Bamiyan

The remains of two giant statues known as "the Buddhas of Bamiyan" lie in the Bamiyan Valley. The statues were carved out of sandstone cliffs from about 100 to 400 A.D. They were covered in a mixture of mud and straw that was molded to create each Buddha's face, hands, and the folds of his robe. Then, they were plastered, painted, and decorated with elaborate ornaments. Over time, the details on the statues wore away and the paint faded because of the wind and rain.

In 1998, the Taliban, who were destroying all artwork and **artifacts** that were not Muslim, dynamited and fired rockets at the Buddhas. They destroyed one Buddha's face and the folds of the other Buddha's robes. In 2001, the Taliban almost completely destroyed what remained of the statues.

(above) The name Shar-i-Gholghola means "City of Sighs." When people lived in the city, they used to climb up tall cliffs from which they could see the Buddhas of Bamiyan. The sight was so breathtaking that people's sighs could be heard everywhere.

Shar-i-Gholghola

Shar-i-Gholghola was a city in the Bamiyan Valley. **Archaeologists** believe that sand dunes, which rise to heights of more than 66 feet (eighteen meters) and move six inches (fifteen centimeters) in one day, covered the city and forced people to leave. Shar-i-Gholghola's ruins, which include a citadel that is surrounded by a 49-foot- (fifteen-meter-) tall wall and three moats, are well preserved beneath the sand.

Outside the northern town of Tashkurghan are two large chunks of rock, all that remains of an ancient stone wall and gate that once surrounded the town.

On the northern plains

Muslims enter the Blue Mosque in Mazar-e-Sharif for morning prayer. According to Islam, Muslims must pray five times a day.

On the northern plains of Afghanistan is the town of Mazar-e-Sharif, which means "Noble Grave" in Dari. It is famous for its many tombs and shrines. The tomb of Ali marks the place where Muslims believe Ali, the cousin and son-in-law of the prophet Muhammad, is buried. It stands inside the Blue Mosque, which is decorated with hundreds of thousands of blue tiles. Another tomb houses the remains of the poet Rabia Balkhi, who died in 955 A.D. Balkhi was the first woman to write love poetry in the **Persian** language. According to legend, she killed herself when her brother forbade her from marrying a slave with whom she had fallen in love. Balkhi wrote her last poem with her own blood. Men and women visit the tomb to pray for success in love.

Surrounding Mazar-e-Sharif is a fertile region where farmers grow cotton, grain, and fruit, such as melons. Wheat is made into flour at the city's flour mills. Mazar-e-Sharif's other main industries, are manufacturing textiles, such as cotton and silk, processing the skins and wool of Karakul sheep, and creating handmade rugs.

Balkh

Balkh is a small town in northern Afghanistan, near Mazar-e-Sharif. In the third century B.C., it was the headquarters of Alexander the Great's Macedonian Empire. At the time, it was called Bactria. By the first century A.D., Bactria was a center for Buddhism. **Monasteries** and *stupas*, which are dome-shaped shrines in which holy items are stored, were built there. In the 700s, Arabs conquered Bactria and made the city a center of learning. Soon, Bactria became known as "Balkh," which means "Mother of all Cities."

Balkh was destroyed in 1221, but rebuilt in the early 1400s. The Khaja Mohammed Parsa, a mosque covered in bright blue ceramic tiles, still stands from this time, along with the ruins of the Arch of Nawbahar, which was part of the walls that once surrounded the city. Some of the walls and columns of the Madjide Haji Pivada, one of the oldest mosques in the world, are also in Balkh. The Madjide Haji Pivada was built in the 800s.

The ruins of an ancient palace stand in Balkh.

Desert cities, past and present

The desert village of Chugha was abandoned after long periods of war.

Cars, trucks, bicycles, and three-wheeled vehicles called tuc tucs *travel along the streets of Kandahar. The drivers of* tuc tucs, *which are like taxis, sit in the front seat, while passengers sit in the back.*

With the whipping winds, long periods of **drought**, and extremely hot and cold temperatures, it is surprising that anyone would live in the desert, but many people do. Over hundreds of years, towns and cities have popped up all over the desert. Some of these towns and cities still exist, but many others were abandoned because of poor weather conditions that made the land impossible to farm, or because of war. As time passed, the swirling sands of the deserts swept over the abandoned cities, covering them almost completely.

Kandahar

Kandahar is a city in the southeastern desert that is surrounded by fertile farmland and irrigated fields where melons, grapes, and other fruit grow. It was once a main stopping point for merchants, especially people who traded arts and crafts from India and Iran. Kandahar was also the country's first capital from 1774 to 1776, during the rule of Ahmad Shah. Today, Kandahar is Afghanistan's second largest city. In its many bazaars, people sell grains; fruit; sheep, goats, and other livestock; and fabrics, such as silk, felt, and wool.

Tombs and shrines

A mausoleum, or tomb, built in Kandahar honors Afghanistan's first king, Ahmad Shah. The blue dome of Ahmad Shah's Maqbara, also called Ahmad Shah's Ziarat, looms high above Kandahar. Each year, thousands of people visit this mausoleum.

People in Kandahar also visit a shrine called the Kharka Sharif, which holds a cloak that Afghans believe once belonged to the prophet Muhammad. According to one legend, Ahmad Shah found the cloak in Bukhara, a city in present-day Uzbekistan. He wanted to take the cloak to Kandahar, but knew that the owners would never allow him to do so. Instead, he asked if he could borrow the cloak, and promised that he would never take it far from a giant rock nearby.

When the owners agreed, Ahmad Shah had the rock dug out of the ground and took it to Kandahar with the cloak. Today, the rock stands outside the shrine.

Herat

The city of Herat is in the western desert, on the Hari River. It is an important stop on the trade route to Iran. Herat's main industries are carpet and fabric weaving, and producing small detailed paintings, known as miniatures, which depict scenes from history and **folklore**.

(top) A young boy sits on a wall overlooking a mosque in Herat and watches people gather in the courtyard after the early morning prayer.

The rebuilding of Herat

Beginning in 329 B.C., Herat was conquered, destroyed, and rebuilt several times. In the 1400s and 1500s, the city became a center for Persian art, architecture, and learning. Remains of many of Herat's ancient buildings can still be seen, including parts of the walls and gate that once surrounded the city. Inside the walls is the Masjid-i-Jami, or Friday Mosque, which is covered with intricate tile work. The mosque has been damaged by fighting and restored several times.

The *musalla* complex

In the late 1400s, Queen Gowhar Shad built a *madrassa*, or place of learning, and a *musalla*, or place of worship, in Herat. All that remains of these buildings are six of the original twelve minarets, which are tall towers from which worshipers are called to prayer. Queen Gowhar Shad's tomb still stands in the complex, although its blue paneled tiles and inscriptions with passages from the *Qur'an*, the Muslim holy book, have been damaged over time. In February 2001, the United Nations decided to fund a project to restore the *musalla* complex and build gardens on the site.

Bust

The modern city of Lashkargah was built on the site of the ancient city of Bust, in the Registan Desert. During the 1000s and 1100s, Bust, also called Kalah Bust, was a winter resort and hunting grounds for rulers of the Ghaznavid Empire. At the top of a mound stood the Qulca-i-Bust citadel. People used to enter the citadel through an arch covered in a brightly colored **mosaic**. The arch still stands at the foot of the mound.

The remains of ancient bazaars, palaces, baths, and mosques have been found near the arch at Qulca-i-Bust.

Farming and herding

Most people in Afghanistan make their living by herding goats, sheep, and yaks, and by farming, even though much of the rugged land is not suitable for growing crops. With **irrigation** systems, farmers can grow crops in areas where there are no rivers or where rivers dry up because of droughts.

Living off the land

Most farmers do not own their own land. Instead, they rent small farming plots or work together on larger farms, giving the landlord a percentage of the crops they grow. The remainder of the crops are taken to processing plants where they are made into other products. For example, wheat is made into flour and sugar cane is made into sugar. Farmers also take their harvested crops to bazaars, where they barter, or trade, them for fabric, sugar, tea, and other items they need.

(right) A farmer and his son winnow their wheat harvest. Winnowing is separating the wheat's chaff, which cannot be eaten, from the grain by throwing the wheat into the air. The light chaff blows away in the wind while grain drops back to the ground where it is later collected.

(below) Plows pulled by oxen prepare the land for farming.

What to grow

The most common crop in Afghanistan is wheat, which is grown in many regions. Cotton planted in the north and southwest is used to make fabric that is sold in Afghanistan and other countries. Rice paddies, or fields, fill the terraces of the Hindu Kush near Jalalabad. In lush valleys in the east, apples, pears, apricots, plums, cherries, pomegranates, grapes, and melons grow. Sugar cane also grows in the east, while sugar beets, which are eaten or made into sugar, are harvested in the north. Nuts, such as almonds, pistachios, and walnuts, grow throughout the country.

A sheep is sheared at a livestock market in Kabul before being sold or traded.

Poppies

Poppies are a flower from which legal drugs, such as morphine, and illegal drugs, such as heroin and opium, are made. Poppies are easy to grow because they require very little water. During Taliban rule, many farmers grew poppies even though it was illegal because they earned a lot of money from their sale. Some farmers even converted fields that grew food crops into poppy fields in the hope of earning a better living. Many Afghans went hungry because there was less food.

Today, other countries and the government of Afghanistan are helping Afghan farmers turn their poppy fields back into fields that grow food. They are giving Afghan farmers seeds that will grow in the country's harsh conditions. They are also helping Afghans repair irrigation systems destroyed by years of war and remove landmines so that farmers can work the land once again.

Farmers are beginning to use modern equipment to plant new crops in fields where poppies once grew.

Livestock

In parts of Afghanistan that are too rocky or too high for farming, people raise livestock, such as Karakul sheep, goats, and yaks. These animals have cloven, or hoofed, feet that allow them to climb through the mountains in search of grazing land. People use the pelts, or skins, of Karakul sheep and goats to make heavy coats, and they eat the animals' meat. They also drink and make cheese from yaks' milk, and weave yaks' hair into blankets, carpets, and fabric for clothing. In places where the land is not as rugged, farmers raise cattle for their milk.

Industries

Industry in Afghanistan, especially through the years of fighting, has not had a chance to develop and modernize. Most Afghan industries are based on agriculture. Fabric is made in cotton textile plants, and leather for clothing is produced in tanning plants. Many small industries, such as machine repair shops, bakeries, and soap, shoe, and ceramics factories, were forced to shut down during Taliban rule. People had to survive on very little, and many made a living by trading crops they grew on farms or items they owned. Since the fall of the Taliban, new shops and businesses are opening, and larger industries are beginning to operate again.

Factories that were closed during Taliban rule are operating once again.

Carpet weaving

Afghan carpets are sold in bazaars throughout the country and in countries around the world. The beautiful carpets are woven by hand or on machines called looms. The carpets are decorated with patterns that have been passed down from generation to generation. Some patterns are geometric, while others show images from nature, such as flowers, or scenes from everyday life.

To make the carpets, wool shorn from sheep or goats is divided into piles based on color. Ivory-colored wool is the most valued because it is easiest to dye, followed by tan, gray, and brown wool. The wool is dyed with vegetables and **minerals**. Popular colors for rugs are red, black, and green. Green represents Islam and is present in many forms of Afghan art. Some of the finest Afghan carpets are made in Meymaneh, in northwestern Afghanistan. These carpets have the tiniest knots arranged in the most detailed patterns. They take months to weave and are very expensive to buy.

Metalwork and jewelry

Afghan metalworkers make plows, shovels, pickaxes, and knives from sheets of iron. Coppersmiths produce pots, trays, and jugs, which they decorate with elaborate patterns or beautiful writing called calligraphy. Jewelers create silver and gold rings, bracelets, pins, and necklaces using techniques that are hundreds of years old. Some jewelry is inscribed with verses from the *Qur'an*, while other pieces are decorated with beads and old coins.

Three women weave a carpet on a loom so large that it must be used outside.

One hump or two?

One- and two-humped camels live in Afghanistan. Dromedaries, which have one hump, are commonly seen on Afghanistan's plains. Bactrian camels, which have two humps, live in the mountains. They weigh up to 1,500 pounds (680 kilograms), and have hair on their humps, chins, shoulders, and hind legs. This hair becomes thicker in the winter, which allows the camels to survive the cold temperatures. Both types of camels are mainly used for transportation, but some are raised as livestock and used for their hair, meat, and milk.

Endangered animals

Many species of animals in Afghanistan are hunted for their furs, horns, and meat. Laws are being put in place to protect certain species, but some animals are still threatened with **extinction**. Snow leopards in the northeastern mountains are hunted for their furs, which are used to make coats, hats, and rugs. Marco Polo sheep are also endangered. These sheep, which are named after the Italian explorer who traveled through Afghanistan on his way to China, are hunted for their long, curling horns which grow to be almost five feet (1.5 meters) long.

Brown bears have very long, straight claws which they use to dig up roots to eat.

It is estimated that only 100 to 200 snow leopards are left in Afghanistan. The animals are hard to count because they live high in the mountains and hide from people.

Glossary

ally A country that officially supports another, especially during a war

archaeologist A person who studies the past by looking at buildings and artifacts

artifact A product, usually historical, made by human craft

caravan A group of travelers journeying together, often for safety reasons

citadel A fortress that commands a city

civilization A society with a well-established culture that has existed for a long time

communist Relating to an economic system where the country's natural resources, businesses, and industry are owned and controlled by the government

coup The overthrow of a government

drought A long period of time when no rain falls

dynasty A family or group of rulers that stays in power for a long time

evaporate To change from a liquid into a gas

extinction The state of no longer being in existence, as with certain species of animals

fertile Able to produce abundant crops or vegetation

folklore The traditional beliefs, stories, and customs of a group of people that have been passed down through generations by word of mouth

homeland A country that is identified with a particular people or ethnic group

invader A person who enters using force

irrigation The supplying of water to land

livestock Farm animals

mineral A naturally occurring, non-living substance obtained through mining

monastery A building where monks live and work according to religious rules

mosaic A design made from small tiles or stones

mosque A Muslim house of worship

nomadic Having no fixed home and moving from place to place in search of food and water

Persian Relating to the country, now called Iran, that is west of Afghanistan

plain A large area of flat land

prophet A person who is believed to speak on behalf of God

refugee A person who leaves his or her home or country because of danger

shaft A long, deep hole

shrine A small area or structure dedicated to a god or saint

terrorist A person who uses violence to intimidate a society or government

tributary A body of water feeding a larger body of water

United Nations An international organization that promotes peace

 # Index

1 2 3 4 5 6 7 8 9 0   Printed in the USA   0 9 8 7 6 5 4 3